HENRY
FORD

BOOK FOR CURIOUS KIDS

Exploring the Ingenious Mind
Behind the Automobile
Revolution

ERIC LYLANI

ERIC LYLANI

TABLE OF CONTENTS

INTRODUCTION

Have you ever wondered what it takes to change the world? How does a young, curious mind evolve into a visionary who transforms entire industries? Join us on a captivating journey through the life and legacy of one of history's greatest innovators—Henry Ford.

In this book, we delve into the remarkable story of Henry Ford, a man whose insatiable curiosity and determination led him to revolutionize transportation, manufacturing, and modern living. From humble beginnings to global recognition, Henry Ford's life is a testament to the power of perseverance, creativity, and the relentless pursuit of dreams.

Each chapter unfolds a new chapter in Henry Ford's life, filled with adventure, challenges, and groundbreaking discoveries. Discover how a young boy's fascination with machines evolved into the creation of the iconic Model T. Explore the innovations that forever changed the way cars were manufactured, making them accessible to millions.

Follow Henry Ford's journey as he navigates through hard times, wartime contributions, and the quest for innovation. Learn about the supportive individuals who shaped his life and the battles he faced in the business world.

Through anecdotes, stories, and fascinating facts, we uncover the hidden layers of Henry Ford's life—from his relationship with his son Edsel to his collaborations with Thomas Edison. Join us as we unravel the man behind the legend and celebrate his enduring impact on industry and society.

Whether you're a young reader with a passion for invention or someone curious about the history of innovation, this book invites you to explore the life of Henry Ford—a pioneer whose legacy continues to inspire generations.

Get ready to embark on an extraordinary journey through history, innovation, and Henry Ford's remarkable legacy. Welcome to the world of curiosity, determination, and the spirit of endless possibilities. Let's dive in!

ERIC LYLANI

A Curious Beginning

In the quiet countryside of Greenfield Township, Michigan, Henry Ford came into the world on July 30, 1863. He was the firstborn of William and Mary Ford, a hardworking farming couple. From the start, young Henry showed a keen interest in the world of machines.

Growing up on a farm, Henry was surrounded by the sights and sounds of agricultural machinery. He often watched the steam-powered tractors and threshing machines in action, marveling at their efficiency and power. This early exposure sparked his curiosity about how things worked.

Henry was not content to simply observe. He was a hands-on learner, always eager to experiment and tinker. At the age of 12, he received his first pocket watch. Instead of just telling time, this watch became Henry's gateway into the fascinating world of mechanics. He took it apart and put it back together countless times, learning about gears, springs, and precision.

As he grew older, Henry's fascination with machines continued to grow. He would spend hours studying the inner workings of steam engines and other mechanical devices. He frequented local machine shops, where he absorbed knowledge from skilled craftsmen and engineers.

Despite his interest in machinery, Henry also embraced the joys of farm life. He helped his father with daily chores, gaining a strong work ethic and practical skills. He enjoyed riding horses, fishing in the nearby river, and exploring the woods with his siblings and friends.

A blend of hard work and youthful curiosity marked Henry's childhood. His experiences on the farm taught him the value of perseverance and problem-solving. Meanwhile, his passion for machines laid the foundation for his future endeavors in engineering and innovation.

ERIC LYLANI

Mastering Watch Repair

As a young boy, Henry showed a knack for fixing things. He was fascinated by the intricate gears and tiny parts inside a watch. When his friends or family had broken watches, they would turn to Henry for help.

What made Henry's watch repairs so special was that he made his own tools. He didn't have fancy equipment or expensive kits. Instead, Henry used whatever he could find—a piece of metal here, a small file there—to craft tools that fit the job perfectly.

Henry's workshop was a sight to behold. Tucked away in a corner of his family's farm, it was filled with bits of metal, gears, and tiny tools. Henry would spend hours carefully disassembling watches, studying how they worked, and then putting them back together again, good as new.

His friends marveled at Henry's skills. They would bring him their broken pocket watches, and Henry would work his magic. With steady hands and a keen eye, he would diagnose the problem, gently coaxing the watch back to life.

Repairing watches wasn't just a hobby for Henry—it was a way to learn about machines and craftsmanship. Each repair taught him something new about mechanics and precision.

Henry's passion for fixing watches foreshadowed his future as an inventor. He dreamed of building machines that could change the world, just like the watches he repaired changed people's lives.

But no matter where life took him, Henry never forgot the lessons he learned from repairing watches. His experience as a young watch repairman taught him patience, attention to detail, and the joy of solving problems.

ERIC LYLANI

Exploring New Horizons

Life on the farm was filled with adventure and hard work for the young boy. He spent his days helping his family tend to the crops and care for the animals. But when tragedy struck, and his beloved mother passed away in 1876, everything changed.

Ford was devastated by his mother's death. His father, expecting him to take over the family farm eventually, hoped he would find solace in continuing their agricultural legacy. However, the young boy harbored a deep dislike for farm work. He later reflected, "I never had any particular love for the farm— it was the mother on the farm I loved."

Driven by a desire to escape the life that held painful memories, the boy made a bold decision. He packed his bags and bid farewell to the familiar sights of the countryside. His destination? The bustling city of Detroit.

In Detroit, the boy sought to learn more about the machines that fascinated him. He found an opportunity to start an apprenticeship at a machine shop. This was a big step for the young apprentice, leaving behind the quiet farm life for the vibrant energy of the city.

At the machine shop, he soaked up knowledge like a sponge. He learned how to operate different tools and machines, gaining practical skills that would serve him well in the years to come. The boy's enthusiasm and determination impressed his mentors, who recognized his potential.

Life in the city was vastly different from the farm. The streets were busy with people and carriages, and factories hummed with activity. Despite the challenges of adjusting to city life, the young apprentice embraced the opportunities for growth and learning.

As he honed his skills at the machine shop, the apprentice's passion for engineering and invention continued to blossom. He experimented with new ideas and techniques, eager to make his mark in the world of machines.

The boy's journey from the farm to the city marked the beginning of an exciting chapter in his life. Little did he know that this apprenticeship would lay the groundwork for groundbreaking innovations that would shape the future of transportation.

With determination and a thirst for knowledge, the young apprentice embarked on a path that would lead him to greatness. And so, the story of his remarkable journey was just getting started...

Discovering a World of Machines

After settling into life in Detroit, the young apprentice's fascination with machines only grew stronger. He was like a detective on a mission to uncover the secrets of how things worked.

Every spare moment was spent exploring the inner workings of engines and machines. He visited workshops and factories, watching skilled craftsmen at work. His eyes sparkled with curiosity as he learned about gears, belts, and engines that powered the city.

Back in his small workshop, the apprentice started experimenting with his own inventions. Using scraps of metal and spare parts, he built simple contraptions to test his ideas. Sometimes, they worked beautifully; other times, they fell apart with a clatter!

One day, he had a brilliant idea. He wanted to build a machine that could move on its own, powered by something more than just muscle. With determination, he set to work, sketching out plans and gathering materials.

After many trials and errors, he finally succeeded. His creation sputtered and rattled, but it moved forward! It was a thrilling moment for the young inventor. He had built his very own self-propelled vehicle—a small prototype of what would become a lifelong passion.

As he shared his achievements with others, the young apprentice gained a reputation for his ingenuity and determination. People started to take notice of his talent and potential.

The world of engines and machines was like a puzzle waiting to be solved, and the young apprentice was determined to unlock its secrets. With each experiment, he learned valuable lessons and gained new skills.

With his eyes fixed on the future, the young inventor continued to explore, imagine, and create. And so, the story of his remarkable journey was taking shape—one invention at a time.

ERIC LYLANI

A Bright Opportunity

In the bustling city of Detroit, Henry Ford was about to embark on an exciting new chapter in his life. It was the year 1891, and Henry had just landed a job at the Edison Illuminating Company—a company founded by the renowned inventor Thomas Edison.

Henry was thrilled to join Edison's company. He saw this as a golden opportunity to learn from one of the greatest inventors of all time. His passion for machines and engines had led him to this moment, and he was eager to soak up knowledge like a sponge.

At the Edison Illuminating Company, Henry's days were filled with hands-on experiences and valuable lessons. He worked diligently, absorbing everything he could about electricity, generators, and power distribution systems. He was fascinated by the transformative impact of electricity on people's lives.

One of the most exciting aspects of working at Edison's company was the chance to interact with Thomas Edison himself. Henry admired Edison greatly and saw him as a role model. He seized every opportunity to learn directly from the legendary inventor.

Edison, impressed by Henry's enthusiasm and curiosity, took him under his wing. He recognized Henry's potential and encouraged him to pursue his ideas and inventions. Henry soaked up Edison's wisdom like a thirsty plant absorbing water.

During his time at the Edison Illuminating Company, Henry gained valuable insights into innovation and problem-solving. He learned the importance of persistence and experimentation—qualities that would later define his own approach to invention.

One day, Henry had an idea that he couldn't shake off. He envisioned a world where every household could have its own source of power—a dream that seemed far-fetched at the time. Inspired by Edison's ingenuity, Henry began to experiment with ways to make this dream a reality.

As Henry continued to learn and grow at the Edison Illuminating Company, he also honed his skills as a mechanic and engineer. His experiences there laid a strong foundation for his future endeavors in the automotive industry.

But Henry's journey was not without challenges. Like any aspiring inventor, he faced setbacks and obstacles along the way. However, he never lost sight of his goals, fueled by the knowledge and inspiration he gained from his time at Edison's company.

By the time Henry left the Edison Illuminating Company in 1899, he was filled with a newfound sense of purpose and determination. His time working alongside Thomas Edison had ignited a spark within him—a spark that would soon ignite a revolution in transportation.

The Birth of a Marvelous Machine

In the year 1896, in the bustling city of Detroit, Henry Ford was on the brink of an extraordinary breakthrough. Inspired by his fascination with machines and engines, Henry set out to create something revolutionary—the first gasoline-powered automobile.

Henry's vision was bold and ambitious. He dreamed of building a vehicle that could move without the need for horses or steam engines. With determination and a relentless spirit of innovation, he embarked on a journey that would change the course of history.

Using the skills and knowledge he gained from working with Thomas Edison and his experiences at the Edison Illuminating Company, Henry began experimenting with different designs and components. He envisioned a compact, lightweight vehicle that could run on gasoline—a novel idea at the time.

Henry faced many challenges along the way. One of the biggest hurdles was finding the right engine for his automobile. Gasoline engines were still in their infancy, and reliable parts were hard to come by. Undeterred, Henry worked tirelessly, often late into the night, to overcome these obstacles.

After more than two years of experimentation, on June 4, 1896, in a tiny workshop behind his home on 58 Bagley Avenue, Detroit, Henry Ford put the finishing touches on his pure ethanol-powered motor. At the age of 32, he completed his first experimental automobile, which he proudly named the "Quadricycle."

The Ford Quadricycle was a simple yet ingenious invention. It consisted of a frame mounted with a gas-powered engine, supported by four bicycle wheels. This unique design captured the imagination of those who witnessed it.

On that historic day, Henry test-drove the Quadricycle, achieving a top speed of 20 mph (32 km/h)—an impressive feat for the time. The little vehicle, though rudimentary, marked a significant milestone in automotive history.

The earliest cars, like Henry's Quadricycle, were hand-built one by one and considered toys for the wealthy. In the 1890s, the concept of a "horseless carriage" was still evolving, and there was no universal idea of what a car should look like or how it should function. Inventors like Henry Ford were pioneers, shaping the future of transportation with their imaginations and ingenuity.

The success of the Quadricycle inspired Henry to pursue further advancements in automobile engineering. In 1899, it led to the founding of the Detroit Automobile Company, followed by the Henry Ford Company in 1901, and ultimately, the establishment of the iconic Ford Motor Company in 1903.

The Quadricycle featured a two-cylinder engine capable of producing four horsepower. It was driven by a chain and had a transmission with two gears—first for speeds up to 10 mph (16 km/h) and second for speeds up to 20 mph (32 km/h). Notably, the vehicle did not have a reverse gear and was steered using a tiller.

Today, the original Quadricycle resides at The Henry Ford Museum in Dearborn, Michigan, a testament to Henry Ford's pioneering spirit and his pivotal role in revolutionizing the automotive industry.

ERIC LYLANI

A Dream Takes Shape

In 1903, a monumental event unfolded in Detroit, Michigan—the founding of the Ford Motor Company by the visionary inventor Henry Ford. This marked a pivotal moment in automotive history and set the stage for groundbreaking innovations that would revolutionize transportation.

Henry Ford had long been passionate about automobiles and was determined to make them accessible to everyone, not just the wealthy. Armed with his experience and ingenuity, Henry took a bold step forward by establishing his own company dedicated to manufacturing automobiles.

The early days of the Ford Motor Company were filled with excitement and challenges. Henry envisioned a future where cars were affordable and practical for ordinary people. To achieve this vision, he needed to develop efficient manufacturing methods that could produce vehicles on a large scale.

One of Henry's key contributions to the automotive industry was the implementation of the moving assembly line—an innovative production method that revolutionized manufacturing. This allowed Ford Motor Company to produce cars more quickly and cost-effectively than ever before.

Despite his innovative ideas, Henry faced skepticism and resistance from traditionalists in the industry. Many believed that automobiles were luxury items reserved for the elite. However, Henry remained steadfast in his belief that cars could be a practical mode of transportation for everyday use.

The early years of the Ford Motor Company were not without their struggles. Henry encountered financial challenges and setbacks as he worked to establish his business. At one point, he faced significant debts and pressure from investors.

But Henry's determination and resilience proved to be the driving force behind his success. He was not afraid to take risks and challenge conventional thinking. With each obstacle he faced, Henry emerged stronger and more determined to achieve his goals.

In 1908, the Ford Motor Company introduced the Model T—an affordable, reliable car that would forever change the automotive landscape. The Model T was a triumph of innovation and efficiency, designed to meet the needs of everyday people.

The popularity of the Model T soared, and demand for Ford cars grew rapidly. Henry's commitment to mass production and affordability made Ford Motor Company a leader in the automotive industry.

One of the most significant milestones for Henry Ford and his company was the introduction of the $5 workday in 1914. This bold move doubled the wages of Ford's factory workers and reduced the workday to eight hours. It was a revolutionary decision that improved the lives of Ford employees and set a new standard for labor practices.

Despite the success of the Model T and the implementation of the assembly line, Henry was not content to rest on his laurels. He continued to innovate and improve his cars, always striving to make transportation more accessible and efficient.

The Ford Motor Company's legacy extends far beyond the cars it produced. Henry Ford's commitment to innovation, affordability, and social responsibility left an indelible mark on the automotive industry and society as a whole.

ERIC LYLANI

A Car for Everyone

After founding the Ford Motor Company in 1903, Henry Ford set out to fulfill his vision of creating an affordable, reliable car for the masses. He believed that everyone should have access to the freedom and convenience of automobile ownership.

Henry assembled a team of talented engineers and designers to develop his dream car, the Model T. Their goal was to design a simple, durable, and easy-to-maintain vehicle. They also aimed to streamline the manufacturing process to make the car affordable for the average American family.

The development of the Model T was a meticulous process that involved countless experiments and iterations. Henry Ford was deeply involved in every aspect of the car's design, from the engine to the chassis to the assembly methods.

Finally, in 1908, after years of hard work and dedication, the first Model T rolled off the assembly line. It was a momentous occasion that marked the beginning of a new era in automotive history.

The Model T quickly captured the hearts and imaginations of Americans from all walks of life. Its affordability, durability, and practicality made it an instant success.

One of the key factors that contributed to the Model T's popularity was its innovative assembly line production method. Henry

Ford implemented a moving assembly line, which allowed for efficient mass production of cars. This significantly reduced manufacturing costs and enabled Ford Motor Company to lower the price of the Model T over time.

The Model T became synonymous with mobility and freedom. It enabled families to travel greater distances and explore new opportunities. Before the Model T, owning a car was considered a luxury reserved for the wealthy. Henry Ford's vision changed that perception, making automobile ownership accessible to the middle class.

As the popularity of the Model T soared, Ford Motor Company faced unprecedented demand for the car. To keep up with production, Henry continuously refined and improved the manufacturing process, introducing new techniques and technologies.

By 1913, Ford Motor Company was producing Model T cars at an astonishing rate. The streamlined production methods allowed them to manufacture more cars in less time, further driving down the cost of the Model T.

The Model T's impact extended beyond transportation. It spurred the growth of industries such as oil and rubber, creating new jobs and economic opportunities. The car also played a role in shaping American culture, contributing to the rise of road trips, suburbanization, and the development of highways.

In addition to its practical benefits, the Model T became a symbol of innovation and progress. Henry Ford's commitment to mass production and affordability revolutionized the automotive industry and set a new standard for manufacturing efficiency.

The Model T's legacy is felt to this day. It laid the foundation for modern automotive engineering and manufacturing practices. Its success inspired generations of carmakers to prioritize efficiency, affordability, and accessibility.

Although production of the Model T eventually ceased in 1927, its impact on American society and culture endures. Henry Ford's vision of making cars "for the great multitude" transformed the way people lived, worked, and traveled.

ERIC LYLANI

The Innovations that Changed Manufacturing Forever

As demand for the Model T soared in the early 1900s, Henry Ford faced a significant challenge—how to meet the growing demand while keeping costs low. Traditional manufacturing methods were slow and labor-intensive, making cars expensive to produce.

Henry Ford believed that efficiency was the key to making cars affordable for the average person. He was determined to streamline the manufacturing process and reduce the time and effort required to build each car.

To achieve this goal, Henry implemented a series of innovative production methods. He studied every step of the manufacturing process, looking for ways to eliminate waste and improve efficiency.

One of Henry's early innovations was the development of interchangeable parts. This concept allowed different components of the car to be manufactured separately and then assembled together, saving time and labor.

Henry also introduced standardized work processes to ensure consistency and quality in car production. By breaking down complex tasks into simpler steps, he made it easier for workers to perform their jobs efficiently.

The most revolutionary innovation pioneered by Henry Ford was the introduction of the moving assembly line in 1913. This innovation transformed the way cars were assembled and significantly reduced production time and costs.

The concept of the moving assembly line was inspired by Henry's observations of meatpacking plants and other industries where goods moved along conveyor belts. He realized that a similar approach could be applied to automobile manufacturing.

In a traditional assembly line, workers would gather all the necessary parts and components before assembling them into a car. This process was slow and required skilled workers to perform multiple tasks.

Henry's moving assembly line changed all that. He arranged workstations along a moving conveyor belt, with each worker responsible for a specific task. As the car chassis moved along the line, workers would add components in a sequential order.

This new method allowed for a continuous flow of production, with cars moving from one workstation to the next at a steady pace. Workers became specialized in their assigned tasks, which increased efficiency and reduced the time required to assemble a car.

The impact of the moving assembly line was profound. It drastically reduced the time it took to build a Model T from over 12 hours to just 93 minutes! This incredible increase in productivity allowed Ford Motor Company to produce cars at a much higher volume and lower cost.

The moving assembly line also significantly impacted the workforce. While some tasks became more repetitive, workers were able to focus on specific tasks and perform them more efficiently, leading to increased wages and job opportunities for many people.

Henry Ford's assembly line innovation revolutionized car manufacturing and influenced industries around the world. The principles of mass production and efficiency introduced by Henry became known as "Fordism" and served as a model for modern industrial practices.

ERIC LYLANI

A Game-Changing Decision

In 1914, something remarkable happened at the Ford Motor Company that would forever change the lives of its workers and set a new standard for industry practices—the implementation of the $5 workday. This bold decision, made by Henry Ford himself, had profound effects on workers and industry standards.

Henry Ford believed in the importance of treating workers well and ensuring they were fairly compensated for their hard work. He understood that happy and well-paid workers would be more productive and loyal to the company.

At the time, factory wages were relatively low, and many workers struggled to make ends meet. Henry Ford recognized the need to address this issue and decided to take action.

In January 1914, Henry Ford made a groundbreaking announcement—he would introduce a minimum wage of $5 per day for all Ford Motor Company employees. This was more than double the average wage for factory workers at the time.

The $5 workday was a significant increase in pay and represented a commitment to improving the quality of life for Ford employees. It was a bold move that attracted attention and sparked discussions across industries.

The implementation of the $5 workday had profound effects on Ford employees and industry standards as a whole.

For Ford workers, the $5 workday brought about immediate improvements in their lives. Many workers experienced a dramatic increase in their standard of living, allowing them to afford better housing, education for their children, and improved healthcare.

The higher wages also boosted morale among Ford employees. Workers felt valued and appreciated by the company, leading to increased job satisfaction and productivity. This, in turn, contributed to higher quality and efficiency in car production.

The $5 workday had ripple effects beyond the Ford Motor Company. Other businesses and industries took note of Henry Ford's progressive approach to labor practices. The concept of paying workers a fair wage for their work gained traction and influenced discussions about workers' rights and labor laws.

Henry Ford's $5 workday set a new standard for industry practices and highlighted the importance of fair compensation and employee welfare. It challenged conventional wisdom about labor costs and productivity, demonstrating that investing in workers could yield positive outcomes for both employees and businesses.

The legacy of Henry Ford's $5 workday extends far beyond its immediate impact on Ford employees. It symbolizes a commitment to social responsibility and equitable treatment of workers.

The Battle of Business

In the bustling world of early automotive innovation, a fascinating clash unfolded between two automotive giants: the Dodge Brothers and Henry Ford. This showdown wasn't just about cars—it was a battle over the very direction of their companies!

Our story begins with Henry Ford, a visionary entrepreneur who revolutionized car manufacturing with the Model T. Ford Motor Company was thriving, but tensions were brewing behind the scenes. Ford wanted to reinvest the company's profits into expanding production and keeping prices low, all while raising wages for his workers.

He believed in spreading the benefits of industrialization to as many people as possible.

On the other side were the Dodge brothers, Horace and John, who supplied parts to Ford Motor Company. They, too, saw the potential of the automobile industry and wanted a bigger piece of the pie. In 1914, the Dodges decided to challenge Ford by launching their own car, the Dodge Model 30, setting the stage for a fierce rivalry.

The turning point came in 1919 when the Dodge brothers filed a lawsuit against Henry Ford. They accused him of mismanaging company funds and prioritizing employees and customers over shareholders. The Michigan Supreme Court, in a landmark decision known as Dodge v. Ford Motor Co., ruled that Ford had to operate the company in the interests of its shareholders rather than solely for social benefits.

This legal battle highlighted a crucial question in corporate law: Should a company prioritize maximizing shareholder wealth above all else? The court's decision affirmed the principle of "shareholder primacy" but also recognized the broad discretion of directors in running a business.

Despite the court's ruling, the feud between Ford and the Dodges continued. Henry Ford threatened to set up a competing manufacturer to pressure his adversaries into selling back their shares. Meanwhile, the Dodge brothers used the funds from the case to expand their own company, fueling further competition in the automotive industry.

Ultimately, the Dodge decision was a mixed outcome for both sides. Ford couldn't unilaterally divert profits away from shareholders, but he retained significant control over his company's direction.

This legendary rivalry sheds light on the complexities of business leadership and corporate governance. It shows that even the most successful entrepreneurs face challenges in balancing competing interests within their companies.

In the end, Henry Ford's vision and the Dodge brothers' ambition left an indelible mark on the automotive world. Their battle for control shaped the course of automotive history, highlighting the importance of responsible management and the pursuit of innovation in business.

A Journey Aboard the Peace Ship

In the midst of World War I, when the world was engulfed in conflict and turmoil, Henry Ford, the visionary founder of Ford Motor Company, embarked on a remarkable mission for peace.

World War I, also known as the Great War, was a devastating conflict that involved many countries and caused immense suffering. As the war raged on, Henry Ford became deeply concerned about the toll it was taking on humanity.

Unlike some industrialists who supported the war effort by producing weapons and military equipment, Henry Ford believed in the power of peace and reconciliation. He felt compelled to take action to end the war and prevent future conflicts.

In 1915, Henry Ford made a bold decision— he would spearhead a peace campaign by organizing a voyage aboard a specially commissioned ship known as the Peace Ship. The goal of this mission was to promote peace and encourage dialogue among warring nations.

The Peace Ship, officially named the "Oscar II," set sail from Hoboken, New Jersey, in December 1915, with Henry Ford and a group of prominent peace advocates on board. The voyage attracted widespread attention and sparked hope for a peaceful resolution to the war.

Henry Ford's presence aboard the Peace Ship was symbolic of his commitment to peace. He believed that diplomacy and dialogue were essential to resolving conflicts and fostering understanding between nations.

During the voyage, Henry Ford and his delegation traveled to Europe with the aim of meeting with world leaders and promoting peace negotiations. However, their efforts were met with skepticism and resistance from some quarters.

Despite facing challenges and setbacks, Henry Ford remained steadfast in his belief that peace was possible. He continued to advocate for diplomacy and non-violent conflict resolution, hoping to inspire change on a global scale.

The Peace Ship voyage captured the imagination of people around the world and ignited discussions about the importance of diplomacy and cooperation in times of crisis. While the war ultimately continued, Henry Ford's efforts to promote peace left a lasting impact on public consciousness.

Although the Peace Ship mission did not achieve its intended goal of ending World War I, Henry Ford's commitment to peace and diplomacy resonated with many people. His advocacy for non-violence and conflict resolution inspired future generations to pursue peaceful solutions to global challenges.

Innovations in Production

As the demand for automobiles continued to rise after World War I, Henry Ford recognized the need to expand production capabilities to meet this growing demand. The Highland Park Plant, located in Michigan, became the focal point of Ford Motor Company's manufacturing operations during this time.

One of the key advancements at the Highland Park Plant was the implementation of the moving assembly line on a larger scale. Henry Ford further refined his assembly line techniques, optimizing workflows and reducing production times.

The Highland Park Plant underwent significant expansion to accommodate increased production capacity. New facilities and assembly lines were added, enabling Ford Motor Company to produce more cars at a faster rate.

The period from 1918 to 1927 marked a period of evolution in production techniques at the Highland Park Plant. Henry Ford and his team continued to experiment and innovate, seeking ways to improve efficiency and reduce costs.

One notable change during this time was the introduction of more specialized machinery and tools. Ford Motor Company invested in new equipment and technologies to automate certain tasks, further streamlining the production process.

The concept of mass production was refined at the Highland Park Plant. Standardization of parts and components allowed for greater interchangeability and reduced the complexity of assembly.

Henry Ford's commitment to efficiency extended beyond the assembly line. He introduced new management practices, including the concept of "scientific management," which emphasized systematic approaches to improving productivity.

The Highland Park Plant became a model of modern manufacturing, attracting attention from industries beyond automotive. Henry Ford's production techniques were studied and adopted by companies seeking to improve their own operations.

The Highland Park Plant's legacy extends beyond its contributions to automotive manufacturing. It symbolizes Henry Ford's relentless pursuit of efficiency and innovation.

The advancements made at the Highland Park Plant laid the groundwork for future developments in manufacturing. Concepts such as mass production, standardization, and automation became fundamental principles in industrial engineering.

The Highland Park Plant also had a profound impact on labor practices. While automation and specialization increased productivity, they also raised questions about the role of workers in an increasingly mechanized world.

A Vision in the Jungle

In 1927, Henry Ford acquired a vast tract of land in the Amazon rainforest of Brazil with the intention of creating a rubber plantation to supply latex for automobile tires. This project was named Fordlandia and was envisioned as a self-contained community where workers would live and work harmoniously.

Fordlandia was established as an experiment in industrial self-sufficiency. The site was designed to replicate an American town, complete with houses, schools, hospitals, and recreational facilities. The goal was to create a model community that would produce rubber efficiently and sustainably.

However, Fordlandia faced numerous challenges from the outset. The harsh conditions of the Amazon rainforest presented logistical and environmental obstacles. The climate was unforgiving, with heavy rains, pests, and diseases that affected both the workers and the rubber trees.

Cultural differences also posed challenges. The indigenous workers, many of whom had lived in the rainforest for generations, had their own customs and way of life that clashed with the planned structure of Fordlandia.

Despite these challenges, Henry Ford remained determined to make Fordlandia a success. He invested heavily in infrastructure and technology, importing American machinery and equipment to boost productivity.

Fordlandia was more than just a rubber plantation—it represented Henry Ford's broader vision of social and industrial progress. He believed in the concept of "Fordism," which emphasized efficiency, standardization, and self-reliance.

Henry Ford envisioned Fordlandia as a self-sustaining community where workers would enjoy a high standard of living and have access to modern amenities. The town included schools, hospitals, a library, and recreational facilities to improve the quality of life for its residents.

Fordlandia also reflected Henry Ford's interest in conservation and environmental stewardship. He advocated for sustainable agriculture and forestry practices, aiming to strike a balance between economic development and environmental preservation.

Despite Henry Ford's best intentions, Fordlandia ultimately faced significant setbacks. The project struggled to achieve economic viability due to the challenges of rubber production in the rainforest and the complexities of managing a remote workforce.

By the mid-1940s, Fordlandia had largely failed to meet its objectives. The rubber trees were susceptible to diseases, and the community faced ongoing issues with sanitation and living conditions. In 1945, Fordlandia was sold back to the Brazilian government, marking the end of Henry Ford's grand experiment in the Amazon.

While Fordlandia was not a commercial success, its legacy endures as a testament to Henry Ford's innovative spirit and commitment to exploring new frontiers beyond automobile manufacturing.

ERIC LYLANI

Surviving Hard Times

The Great Depression, which began with the stock market crash in 1929, had far-reaching effects on economies around the world. The automobile industry, including Ford Motor Company, was not immune to the economic downturn.

As the Depression deepened, demand for automobiles plummeted. Many people could no longer afford to buy new cars, leading to a sharp decline in sales for Ford and other automakers.

Henry Ford, the founder of Ford Motor Company, faced difficult decisions during this period. To cope with shrinking demand, he implemented cost-cutting measures, including reducing production and laying off workers.

Despite the challenges, Henry Ford remained committed to keeping his company afloat and preserving jobs for as many employees as possible. He believed in the importance of maintaining stability and weathering the storm.

Ford Motor Company took several steps to cope with the economic challenges of the Great Depression. One key strategy was diversifying its product offerings to appeal to different market segments.

During the Depression, Ford introduced more affordable models to attract budget-conscious consumers. The company also focused on improving efficiency and reducing manufacturing costs to lower the prices of its cars.

To support its workforce during this difficult time, Ford Motor Company implemented innovative labor practices. While other companies were laying off workers, Ford avoided widespread layoffs by reducing work hours and implementing profit-sharing programs.

Henry Ford's commitment to his employees was reflected in his efforts to provide support and resources to those affected by the Depression. The company established community programs and initiatives to assist families facing financial hardship.

Despite the economic hardships, Ford Motor Company continued to innovate and invest in research and development. Henry Ford believed in the importance of staying ahead of the competition and preparing for future growth.

The Great Depression had a lasting impact on Ford Motor Company and the automotive industry as a whole. The company's ability to adapt and survive during this challenging period demonstrated resilience and resourcefulness.

Ford Motor Company emerged from the Great Depression stronger and more focused on innovation. The lessons learned during this time shaped the company's approach to business and influenced its future strategies.

Contributions to World War II

As World War II erupted in 1939, Ford Motor Company quickly pivoted its production efforts to support the war. Like many other industries, Ford played a crucial role in manufacturing essential equipment and vehicles needed for the war effort.

One of Ford's primary contributions was the production of military vehicles and equipment. Ford factories were retooled to manufacture trucks, jeeps, tanks, and aircraft components for the Allied forces. These vehicles played a vital role in transporting troops, supplies, and equipment during the war.

In addition to military vehicles, Ford Motor Company also manufactured aircraft engines and parts. The company's expertise in mass production and assembly line techniques enabled it to produce large quantities of engines to power Allied aircraft.

Ford's contributions extended beyond manufacturing. The company also supported war-related research and development, collaborating with government agencies and other industries to innovate new battlefield technologies.

Transitioning to war production posed significant challenges for Ford Motor Company. The demand for military vehicles and equipment was unprecedented, requiring rapid expansion of production facilities and workforce.

One of the key challenges was sourcing materials and components amid wartime shortages. Ford had to adapt to changing supply chains and prioritize critical resources needed for military production.

Another challenge was meeting production quotas while maintaining quality and efficiency. Ford implemented innovative production methods, such as the use of assembly lines and standardized parts, to increase output and reduce costs.

The workforce at Ford faced challenges as well. Many employees enlisted in the military, leading to labor shortages in factories. Ford implemented training programs to recruit and train new workers to fill essential roles.

Despite the challenges, Ford Motor Company's dedication to the war effort was unwavering. The company worked tirelessly to meet production targets and contribute to the Allied victory.

The experience gained during wartime production also paved the way for post-war innovations and advancements in automotive technology. Many of the techniques and technologies developed during the war era were adapted for civilian use, contributing to the growth of the automotive industry.

Retirement Years

After decades of leading the Ford Motor Company and pioneering advancements in the automotive industry, Henry Ford officially retired in 1945. His decision to step down from active leadership marked the end of an era but also signaled a time for reflection and new beginnings.

During his retirement years, Henry Ford shifted his focus from day-to-day business operations to other interests, including philanthropy and personal pursuits. He remained involved with the company as an advisor and continued to exert influence on its direction.

In retirement, Henry Ford had the opportunity to reflect on his remarkable achievements and lasting impact on society. His innovations in automobile manufacturing transformed transportation and shaped modern industry.

Henry Ford's most enduring legacy was the development of the assembly line, which revolutionized production methods and made cars more affordable for the average person. His vision of mass production and standardization set new standards for efficiency and productivity.

Beyond automotive innovation, Henry Ford was also known for his progressive labor practices, including the introduction of the $5 workday and profit-sharing programs. He believed in treating workers fairly and investing in their well-being.

Henry Ford's impact extended beyond business. He was a philanthropist who supported various causes, including education, healthcare, and community development. His contributions helped improve the lives of countless individuals and communities.

Henry Ford's retirement symbolized the culmination of a lifelong journey marked by innovation, entrepreneurship, and social responsibility. His legacy continues to inspire generations of inventors, innovators, and business leaders around the world.

One of Henry Ford's lasting contributions was the Ford Foundation, established in 1936 with a mission to advance human welfare. The foundation supported initiatives in education, healthcare, and economic development, leaving a positive impact on society.

Henry Ford's vision of progress and innovation lives on through Ford Motor Company, which remains a global leader in automotive technology. The company continues to build on Henry Ford's legacy of innovation, sustainability, and mobility.

Henry Ford's Later Years and Passing

Henry Ford's later years were marked by both challenges and transitions within Ford Motor Company. After his son, Edsel Ford, passed away from cancer in May 1943, Henry, now elderly and facing health issues, decided to step back into a leadership role within the company.

At nearly 80 years old, Henry Ford's health was declining, and he struggled with cardiovascular issues that affected both his physical and mental well-being. Despite concerns from many directors about his ability to lead, Henry Ford assumed the presidency of Ford Motor Company once again. Throughout his career, he had always wielded significant influence within the company, and this period was no exception.

During Henry's return to the presidency, Ford Motor Company faced significant financial challenges, with losses exceeding $10 million each month. The administration of President Franklin Roosevelt even considered a government takeover to ensure continued war production, highlighting the seriousness of the situation.

Realizing his limitations, Henry Ford eventually passed the torch to his grandson, Henry Ford II, in September 1945, relinquishing the company presidency and retiring from active leadership.

On April 7, 1947, Henry Ford passed away at his estate in Dearborn, known as Fair Lane, due to a cerebral hemorrhage at the age of 83. His death was mourned by many, and thousands of people paid their respects at a public viewing held at Greenfield Village. The funeral services took place at Detroit's Cathedral Church of St. Paul, and Henry Ford was laid to rest in the Ford Cemetery in Detroit.

Henry Ford's legacy lives on through his innovations and contributions to the automotive industry. His impact continues to be felt worldwide, and he remains a celebrated figure in history, remembered for his pioneering spirit and vision for progress.

ERIC LYLANI

Transforming Industry and Society

Henry Ford's legacy is built upon a foundation of groundbreaking inventions and innovations that transformed the automotive industry and left an indelible mark on society.

One of Ford's most enduring innovations was the development of the assembly line. By introducing a moving assembly line in his factories, Ford revolutionized manufacturing processes, significantly reducing production time and costs. This innovation made cars more affordable and accessible to the general public, sparking a transportation revolution.

Another lasting contribution was Ford's implementation of mass production techniques and standardization. Ford Motor Company became a model of efficiency, producing vehicles with interchangeable parts on a large scale. This approach set new standards for industrial production and influenced manufacturing practices across industries.

Ford's commitment to innovation extended beyond manufacturing. He was instrumental in advancing automotive technology, introducing features like the electric starter, which made cars easier and safer to operate. Ford's continuous improvements in design and engineering set benchmarks for the automotive industry.

Henry Ford's innovations had a profound impact on both industry and society, shaping the modern world in numerous ways.

In terms of industry, Ford's assembly line and mass production techniques became fundamental principles of manufacturing. The concepts of efficiency, standardization, and continuous improvement that Ford pioneered revolutionized industrial processes and laid the groundwork for modern production systems.

Ford's innovations also transformed society by making automobiles more accessible to the middle class. The affordability of Ford cars empowered individuals and families with newfound mobility, enabling greater freedom of travel and economic opportunities.

Furthermore, Ford's progressive labor practices, such as the $5 workday and profit-sharing programs, set precedents for fair wages and employee welfare. These practices contributed to improved working conditions and elevated living standards for workers across industries.

Henry Ford's impact extended beyond automotive manufacturing. His philanthropic endeavors, including the establishment of the Ford Foundation, supported initiatives in education, healthcare, and community development, leaving a lasting legacy of social responsibility.

Preserving a Legacy for Generations

The Henry Ford Museum, located in Dearborn, Michigan, was founded by Henry Ford to showcase the history of American innovation and entrepreneurship. It opened its doors to the public on October 21, 1929, during a time of economic uncertainty and change.

Henry Ford envisioned the museum as a place where visitors could explore the evolution of technology, industry, and culture. The museum's exhibits featured a diverse collection of artifacts, ranging from historic vehicles and machinery to household items and Americana.

One of the museum's highlights is the "With Liberty and Justice for All" exhibit, which includes historically significant artifacts such as the Rosa Parks bus and Abraham Lincoln's chair from Ford's Theatre.

The Henry Ford Museum plays a vital role in preserving Henry Ford's legacy and contributions to American society. Through its exhibits and educational programs, the museum provides insights into Ford's innovative spirit and vision.

The museum's collection reflects Henry Ford's passion for innovation and progress. Visitors can see firsthand the evolution of transportation, from the Model T to modern vehicles, and explore the impact of industrialization on daily life.

Beyond automobiles, the museum showcases innovations in communication, agriculture, manufacturing, and design. Exhibits highlight the ingenuity of American inventors and entrepreneurs who shaped the course of history.

In addition to preserving artifacts, the Henry Ford Museum serves as a hub for education and inspiration. It offers educational programs, workshops, and events that engage visitors of all ages in exploring the intersections of history, technology, and culture.

The museum's mission extends beyond its physical walls. It embraces digital initiatives and online resources to reach a global audience and make Ford's legacy accessible to people around the world.

The Henry Ford Museum stands as a testament to Henry Ford's enduring impact on American society and culture. It celebrates his contributions to innovation, entrepreneurship, and philanthropy.

The museum's commitment to preserving history and inspiring future generations underscores the importance of honoring the past while embracing the possibilities of the future. It fosters curiosity, creativity, and a sense of wonder that encourages visitors to explore their own potential.

Remembering Henry Ford

After Henry Ford's death in 1947, the world mourned the loss of a visionary entrepreneur and inventor. However, his legacy lived on through the countless innovations and contributions he made during his lifetime.

Henry Ford's impact on society was recognized posthumously through various honors and accolades. He was celebrated for revolutionizing the automotive industry with the introduction of the assembly line and mass production techniques.

In addition to automotive achievements, Henry Ford was revered for his progressive labor practices, including the implementation of the $5 workday and profit-sharing programs. These initiatives improved the quality of life for workers and set new standards for employee welfare.

Henry Ford's influence extended beyond industry. He was admired for his philanthropy and support of educational initiatives, such as the Ford Foundation, which continues to fund programs that promote social justice, economic opportunity, and community development.

Henry Ford's contributions to automotive and industrial history continue to shape the modern world. His innovations laid the groundwork for advancements in manufacturing, transportation, and technology.

Ford's development of the assembly line transformed the way goods were produced, making them more affordable and accessible to the general public. This approach revolutionized industries beyond automotive, paving the way for modern manufacturing practices.

The impact of Henry Ford's vision is evident in the evolution of the automobile. His pioneering spirit and commitment to innovation inspired future generations of engineers and entrepreneurs to push boundaries and explore new possibilities.

Ford Motor Company remains a global leader in automotive technology and sustainability, building on Henry Ford's legacy of innovation and entrepreneurship. The company continues to develop electric and autonomous vehicles, furthering Henry Ford's vision of mobility for all.

ERIC LYLANI

Fun Facts and Interesting Stories

Henry Ford, the pioneering founder of Ford Motor Company, was not only a visionary inventor and industrialist but also a fascinating individual with many interesting stories and lesser-known facts. Let's explore some fun facts and anecdotes about Henry Ford that highlight his unique personality and achievements.

Early Curiosity

Henry Ford's curiosity about machines and engines started at a young age while growing up on a farm in Michigan. He was fascinated by the mechanical devices used on the farm, such as steam engines and farm equipment.

Ford spent hours tinkering with these machines, taking them apart and putting them back together to understand how they worked. This early interest in mechanics and engineering laid the foundation for his future innovations in the automotive industry.

First Car - The Quadricycle

Henry Ford's first experiment with building a self-propelled vehicle resulted in the creation of the Quadricycle in 1896. This early automobile was a simple contraption consisting of a lightweight frame mounted on four bicycle wheels powered by a small gasoline engine. Ford built the Quadricycle in a small workshop behind his home, demonstrating his hands-on approach to innovation and problem-solving.

Model T Revolution

Henry Ford's most famous achievement was the development and success of the Model T, introduced in 1908. The Model T, also known as the "Tin Lizzie," was the first mass-produced automobile designed for the average American family. Its affordability, durability, and simplicity revolutionized transportation, making car ownership accessible to millions of people and transforming American society.

$5 Workday - Improving Lives

In 1914, Henry Ford made headlines by implementing the $5 workday for his employees, more than doubling the prevailing wage rate. This bold move was motivated not only by a desire to retain skilled workers but also by Ford's belief that paying higher wages would increase workers' purchasing power and stimulate economic growth. The $5 workday not only improved the lives of

Ford's employees but also set a new standard for fair labor practices in the industry.

Love for Innovation - The Moving Assembly Line

Henry Ford's introduction of the moving assembly line in 1913 revolutionized industrial manufacturing. By arranging workers and machinery in a continuous flow, Ford drastically reduced the time it took to assemble a car from hours to minutes. This innovation dramatically increased production speed and efficiency, allowing Ford Motor Company to produce vehicles at a lower cost and pass on savings to customers.

Greenfield Village - Preserving History

Henry Ford's passion for preserving American history led to the creation of Greenfield Village in Dearborn, Michigan.

This living history museum features historic buildings relocated from across the United States, showcasing American life and innovation. Visitors can explore Thomas Edison's laboratory, ride in a Model T, or experience life in a 19th-century farmhouse, offering a unique glimpse into the past.

Peace Ship - Advocating for Peace

During World War I, Henry Ford funded a peace mission known as the Peace Ship. Ford believed that conflicts could be resolved through diplomacy and cooperation rather than warfare. Despite facing criticism and challenges, Ford's commitment to promoting peace through dialogue and negotiation reflected his idealistic vision for a better world.

Unusual Hobbies - Soybean Experimentation

Henry Ford had unconventional hobbies outside of his work in the automotive industry. He was particularly interested in exploring alternative uses for soybeans as a sustainable resource. Ford believed that soybeans could be used to produce plastics, fuel, and other industrial products. He even designed a car with body panels made from soy-based plastic, demonstrating his innovative approach to agricultural and environmental issues.

Anti-War Stance - Pursuit of Harmony

Despite his involvement in war production during World War II, Henry Ford held strong anti-war sentiments. He believed in using technology and innovation to promote peace and improve human welfare. Ford's commitment to social progress and harmony among nations reflected his belief in the power of constructive dialogue and cooperation to address global challenges.

Legacy of Innovation - Inspiring Future Generations

Henry Ford's legacy extends far beyond the automotive industry. His innovative spirit, commitment to efficiency, and vision for a better future continue to inspire entrepreneurs, inventors, and dreamers worldwide. Ford's contributions to manufacturing, labor practices, and philanthropy have left an indelible imprint on modern society, reminding us of the transformative impact of visionary thinking and perseverance.

These fun facts and anecdotes offer a glimpse into the life and legacy of Henry Ford—a remarkable individual whose contributions continue to shape our modern world. Whether it's his revolutionary approach to manufacturing or his vision for a better future, Henry Ford's impact is felt in every aspect of our lives today.

Pursuing Perfection on the Track

In the early 1900s, Henry Ford was not only building cars but also testing their limits on the race track. He saw racing as an opportunity to prove the capabilities of his automobiles, even though he held reservations about the true measure of a car's worth.

One significant moment in Ford's racing career occurred on October 10, 1901, when he defeated Alexander Winton in a race car named "Sweepstakes." This victory was instrumental in Ford's decision to establish the Henry Ford Company, laying the foundation for his future endeavors in the automotive industry.

Ford continued to push the boundaries of speed and performance with stripped-down Model Ts in various races. In 1909, he entered a grueling "ocean-to-ocean" race across the United States, finishing first (although later disqualified). The following year, in 1911, Ford set a one-mile oval speed record at Detroit Fairgrounds with driver Frank Kulick behind the wheel.

Despite his successes on the track, Ford's interest in racing began to wane by 1913. He attempted to enter a modified Model T in the prestigious Indianapolis 500 but withdrew from the race due to rule changes that he felt compromised the integrity of his car. This marked the end of Ford's racing career as he redirected his focus towards the mass production of the Model T and other innovative projects.

In his autobiography, "My Life and Work," Ford expressed skepticism towards racing as a meaningful measure of automotive excellence. He believed that true success lay in transportation efficiency, production innovation, affordability, reliability, and fuel efficiency—values that would benefit society as a whole.

Despite his personal reservations, Ford's impact on auto racing was undeniable. His dedication to improving his cars' performance on the track reflected his relentless pursuit of excellence in all aspects of automobile manufacturing. In recognition of his contributions, Henry Ford was posthumously inducted into the Motorsports Hall of Fame of America in 1996.

ERIC LYLANI

A Supportive Circle

Henry Ford's family was a big part of his life and success. Henry married Clara Bryant, who had been his friend since they were kids growing up near each other in Michigan. Clara understood Henry's dreams and ambitions, supporting him in every way she could. They got married in 1888 and embarked on a journey together filled with adventures and challenges.

Soon after their marriage, Henry and Clara welcomed their only child, Edsel Ford, into the world in 1893. Edsel grew up surrounded by his father's passion for machines and automobiles. He shared Henry's enthusiasm for innovation and design. As Edsel got older, he became more involved in his father's business, bringing his own artistic talents and business acumen to the table.

Henry's family life was intertwined with his work at Ford Motor Company. Clara and Edsel played key roles in expanding the company's reach and refining its designs. Edsel's creative vision helped introduce new models like the Ford Model A following the success of the iconic Model T.

Beyond their roles in the business, the Ford family was committed to giving back to society. Clara Ford supported various charitable causes, focusing on education and community development. She believed in using their wealth for the greater good.

Henry and Clara instilled important values in their son, Edsel, teaching him the importance of hard work, innovation, and social responsibility. Edsel carried on his family's legacy of philanthropy, continuing to support causes that improved people's lives.

Despite their success, the Ford family faced challenges along the way. Henry's strong personality sometimes led to disagreements, but Clara and Edsel provided a steady foundation and support system during difficult times.

Together, the Ford family's story is one of unity, determination, and shared purpose. They believed in using their influence to make a positive impact on society, leaving a lasting legacy that extends far beyond the automotive industry.

ERIC LYLANI

The Relationship Between Edison and Ford

In the bustling streets of 19th and early 20th-century America, two brilliant minds sparked a friendship that would change the course of history. Thomas Edison and Henry Ford, both visionaries in their own right, shared a deep bond built on innovation, friendship, and mutual admiration.

Their story begins in the dawn of electricity and the automobile age. Thomas Edison, known as the "Wizard of Menlo Park," was already a legend in the world of invention. He pioneered the electric light bulb, the phonograph, and countless other innovations that illuminated cities and transformed everyday life.

Meanwhile, Henry Ford was a young, ambitious engineer with a passion for machinery and a dream of making cars accessible to everyone. Inspired by Edison's ingenuity, Ford embarked on a journey to revolutionize transportation.

Their paths first crossed in 1896 when Ford joined the Edison Illuminating Company in Detroit. Working under Edison's company, Ford had the opportunity to witness firsthand the power of electricity and the potential for innovation it held.

As Ford's automotive ambitions grew, so did his friendship with Edison. The two shared a common vision of harnessing technology to improve people's lives. They often exchanged ideas and advice, fueling each other's passion for invention.

One of the most memorable moments in their friendship occurred in 1914 when Edison and Ford embarked on a camping trip with President Warren G. Harding. This adventure, known as the "Vagabonds," became an annual tradition where the trio explored the wilderness, discussed ideas, and relaxed away from the pressures of their respective industries.

Beyond their personal friendship, Edison and Ford collaborated on several projects. Ford admired Edison's commitment to research and development, while Edison admired Ford's practical approach to innovation. Together, they worked on projects related to electric vehicles and battery technology, aiming to create sustainable transportation solutions.

Their friendship endured through triumphs and challenges. Edison supported Ford during the early years of Ford Motor Company, providing guidance and encouragement. In return, Ford honored Edison's legacy by preserving his laboratory at Menlo Park, New Jersey, as a historic site.

As they grew older, Edison and Ford continued to inspire each other and the next generation of inventors. Their legacy lives on in the innovations that shaped the modern world, from electric power to mass-produced automobiles.

Henry Ford's Relationship with Edsel Ford

In the bustling world of cars and innovation, there was a special bond between a father and his son that shaped the course of automotive history. Henry Ford and his son, Edsel Ford, shared a unique relationship filled with challenges and triumphs, all driven by their love for cars and a vision for the future.

As a young boy, Edsel admired his father's passion for engineering and machinery. He grew up watching Henry Ford tinker with machines and dream of building a car that everyone could afford. Edsel soaked up his father's wisdom and learned the ropes of the automotive business from a young age.

By the time Edsel was old enough to join his father's company, Ford Motor Company was already making waves in the industry. Edsel showed a natural talent for business and design, and Henry recognized his son's potential. He groomed Edsel to be his successor, hoping to pass on the reins of the company one day.

Despite their shared love for cars, Henry and Edsel had their differences. Henry was known for his strong-willed nature and determination to do things his way. He often clashed with Edsel over business decisions and company strategy. However, beneath their disagreements, there was a deep respect and admiration between father and son.

Edsel played a pivotal role in Ford Motor Company's success. He championed innovative designs and pushed for higher quality in Ford cars. Under Edsel's leadership, Ford introduced iconic models like the Model A and the luxurious Lincoln brand, expanding the company's reach and reputation.

Henry Ford valued Edsel's contributions but remained deeply attached to his own vision. This tension sometimes strained their relationship, especially as Edsel sought more creative control over the company.

Tragically, Edsel's life was cut short when he succumbed to cancer in 1943. His passing deeply affected Henry, who struggled to cope with the loss of his son and trusted confidant.

In the aftermath of Edsel's death, Henry Ford faced immense pressure to carry on without his son. He eventually resumed the presidency of Ford Motor Company, but the absence of Edsel left a void that could never be filled.

Despite their differences, Henry Ford's relationship with Edsel was defined by a shared commitment to innovation and a passion for automobiles. Their story reminds us that even the greatest achievements are shaped by the bonds of family and the enduring legacy of love and determination.

The Woman Behind the Innovator

In the captivating tale of Henry Ford's life, there shines a remarkable woman whose support and strength played a pivotal role in his journey—the beloved Clara Ford.

Clara Bryant first crossed paths with Henry Ford in the small town of Greenfield, Michigan. They were childhood friends who grew up in neighboring farms. As they matured, their friendship blossomed into a deep and enduring love.

When Henry was just starting his career, Clara stood by his side, offering unwavering support and encouragement. She believed in his dreams and shared his passion for innovation. Together, they faced the challenges and triumphs of building a future centered around automobiles.

Clara was not just a supportive partner; she was also an integral part of Henry's life and work. She managed the household while Henry pursued his ambitious goals. Clara's organizational skills and practical wisdom complemented Henry's visionary ideas.

As Ford Motor Company grew and flourished, Clara played a behind-the-scenes role in its success. She hosted guests, managed social engagements, and provided a steady presence in Henry's life amidst the whirlwind of business.

Despite her husband's fame and the demands of his work, Clara remained humble and down-to-earth. She valued family above all else and ensured that their children received a loving and stable upbringing.

Clara's impact extended beyond the home. She supported charitable initiatives and community projects, embodying the spirit of giving back to society.

In 1888, Henry and Clara tied the knot and embarked on a lifelong journey together. Their marriage was marked by mutual respect, love, and shared values. Clara's calm demeanor balanced Henry's driven personality, creating a harmonious partnership.

Throughout their marriage, Clara remained Henry's confidante and closest companion.

She encouraged him during challenging times and celebrated his successes with genuine joy.

Tragically, Clara's health declined in her later years, leading to her passing in 1950. Her death deeply affected Henry, who mourned the loss of his beloved wife and partner.

CONCLUSION

As we close the pages of this book, we reflect on the incredible journey we've taken through Henry Ford's life and legacy. From his humble beginnings to his lasting impact on industry and society, Henry Ford's story is one of inspiration, innovation, and the power of perseverance.

Throughout these chapters, we've witnessed the curious beginnings of a young boy who tinkered with machines and dreamed of changing the world. We've explored the pivotal moments that shaped his path—the birth of the Model T, the innovations in manufacturing, and the challenges he faced along the way.

Henry Ford's story is not just about cars and factories; it's about the relentless pursuit of dreams and the belief that anything is possible with determination and hard work. His vision transformed the automotive industry, making cars accessible to millions and forever changing the way we live and work.

However, Henry Ford's legacy extends beyond automobiles. It's about innovation, creativity, and the courage to challenge the status quo. It's about the supportive individuals who stood by his side, the battles he fought in the business world, and the lasting impact he had on industry and society.

As we bid farewell to Henry Ford, we carry with us the lessons he taught us—the importance of curiosity, the value of perseverance, and the belief that one person can indeed change the world. His legacy continues to inspire us to dream big, think boldly, and never stop exploring new horizons.

So, let us remember Henry Ford not just as a historical figure but also as a symbol of possibility and potential. Let us honor his memory by continuing to push the boundaries of innovation and strive for a better future.

As we turn the final page of this book, may we carry with us the spirit of Henry Ford— the spirit of curiosity, determination, and the relentless pursuit of greatness. Thank you for joining us on this incredible journey. And remember, the adventure doesn't end here. There are still countless horizons to explore, dreams to chase, and legacies to create. Farewell, but not goodbye.

Made in United States
Troutdale, OR
11/06/2024